Words f
For Those ot Us Who
Still Struggle

Inspirational Quotes, Phrases and Other Enlightening Things

Ms. Linda,

Thanks for all your support! I truly appreciate it. I hope these words touch you & inspire you to continue to grow.

love~

Ervin M. Thomas

DEDICATION

To my loved ones present and past whose legacy
I still carry on my shoulder and in my heart.

CONTENTS

<u>ACKNOWLEDGEMENTS</u>

Special thanks to my daughters for allowing me the amazing role of being their father and for the enlightening in-depth dialogue we so often share. To all my family and friends for putting up with my views on various topics. And to all the students I was able to enlighten through my work as an educator. I have learned a lot from all of you. Thanks for the energy, memories and times shared. Last, thanks to my talented editor for walking with me to the finish line.

<u>INTRODUCTION</u>

My passion for helping others achieve "their" greatness has always provided me with a sense of peace. It's as if my happiness is found in the happiness of others; especially, if I have a role in bringing about that joy. My family and friends often teased me when I was younger about being a professor. I now realize they saw attributes specially gifted to me and as long as I stay true to my purpose I will find wholeness. Many ask, how do you maintain a healthy balance of spirituality, family, work, school and a relationship while chasing after your dreams and aspirations? I truly believe they are all connected, so it shouldn't feel like one has to (or is taking) precedence over the other. Just stay true to your purpose and all things will find their secure spot in your life, without much friction.

This resource was written with us in mind. These words were gathered to assist with getting back to the essence of living righteously and just.

Thank you,

Ervin M. Thomas

How to Use This Book to Assist on Your Journey

From Front to Back: Starting with chapter 1 and ending with chapter 17, the traveler can read the book from beginning to the last page and enjoy the process of enlightenment, evolution and growth. Working through each phase as a stepping stone to the next.

One a Day: Sometimes we just need one dose of inspiration to assist us with navigating through the day- depending on our mood, the area we are struggling in or may just need more clarification in order to successfully cope.

Locate Something to Say: When you're looking for the perfect words to share to help someone in need of a little motivation just grab one from any section to verbally share, jot in a greeting card or post on social media. A few of words of wisdom go a long way.

Meditate Away: The process of growth and reflection can not be rushed. It requires us to sit with words and allow them to speak to us as we manifest their truth. During this process we may organically select words and reside with them for however long it takes to resonate. Writing on sticky notes that cover the home, office and car, or writing on the palm. Whatever method that works to absorb the psalms.

Chapter 1
Awareness

DEAR TRAVELER:

As you reflect on the day's events, I hope they were filled with lessons Taught and Learned, challenges Confronted and Overcome; lives Uplifted and Inspired. Hopefully, you made some sort of difference in someone's life and caused them to feel empowered and loved. If not, evaluate what areas need improving and start again tomorrow. Live selflessly.

Awareness of all things surrounding you externally and flowing through you internally should be acknowledged and over-stood. Allowing you to access a level of consciousness few people are disciplined enough to uncover.

Be wary with whom you share your aspirations for the future. Do not be naive and believe everyone you engage with has your best interest at heart. Most folks have envious spirits and will only speak damnation against you. Guard your dreams ferociously.

Realize that friendship is necessary, nothing but loyalty, unconditional love and support with a side of non-judgment and encouragement will guide you.

Acknowledge the blessings of support or learn a painful lesson.

Never lower your standards to make yourself accessible to someone. They will eventually reveal they never deserved to sit beside you. Then you will have yourself to blame for letting pity and hope rule your decisions.

All thoughts derive from somewhere, yet sometimes their purpose is not clear. How much time are you given when you awake to record a dream before it fades into the land of "lost visions"? Even nightmares need to be studied because of their insight and the life lessons they possess.

Be conscious of the words and actions of the great deceivers who tamper in trickery an attempt to control you. Their role is to plant unrighteous thoughts in your mind and mislead the masses. Keep your eyes open for symbols and signs. The truth shall be revealed in due time.

We have become brainwashed into believing we are in competition with one another. Where is the finish line and how do you know when you have won the challenge? Is it based on how much money or items you are able to hoard?

Until we finally acknowledge it's really not about us, but something greater, we will continue to act as selfish fools fighting to get to the front of the line to nowhere.

Know thyself on a personal, intimate level and in a spiritual nature, until you understand the reality of your existence and the purpose of your life.

Only when you have taken the time to repair your heart to a healthy beat will you be able to love unconditionally.

Acknowledge the present, claim the future and free yourself from the past. It's the only way out of the darkness which has enslaved your thoughts and caused you to be stagnant and complacent.

Stop wondering why you are not with anyone at the moment in an intimate relationship. God has someone specially designed for you, so just be still and know that your souls are linked and your energy will connect one day soon. Take this time with self to get to know you, so that you will be able to effectively introduce yourself to your mate.

Be aware of the condescending, self-righteous person who thinks he/she is so much better than you. This type of person does not want you to prosper because they would then be forced to evaluate their own situation. Choosing a better life would shine light on their unhappiness. They may not yet be ready or willing to face their own truth.

When you comprehend that generations have walked the Earth at some point and have then died and moved on, you must also accept the fact that you are only living at this moment in time, for a moment in time.

One day, you too shall cease to exist in the physical plane. So stop getting frustrated over trivial matters and work towards living a meaningful life where you impact the lives of others through service and positive energy.

Instead of wishing for what you do not have, become a good steward over what God has blessed you with. This is rule #1, which some folks have yet to master; thus, their unhappiness with self persists and their tortured soul continues to drown.

As much as I hate to admit it, each day I am learning it is not about me (go figure). Instead, it is all about the unconditional love given to others without expectation; regardless of circumstance or situation.

When we burn bridges, does it automatically mean we do not have any future intentions of crossing over them again? Try not to start flames that cause too much destruction.

Chapter 2
Forgiveness

DEAR READER:

Have you ever tried your hardest to move in a particular direction of your life only to find yourself months later standing at the same point? You begin wondering why energy is being exerted, but you don't seem to be moving forward at all? I've learned that when we carry around hurt, pain, upset, frustrations and the countless number of other heavy burdens it weighs us down and permits us from flourishing and being overjoyed. We must heal ourselves by releasing all those unnatural energies we've held onto so we can finally fly.

Forgiveness is where our unlocking begins. Releasing oneself from bondage even when others refuse to allow or accept your transition into the realm of freedom.

Yesterday, forgiveness was granted to all those who had done me wrong. Today, I see clearly.

Relinquish all the thoughts of resentment held for decades. They have exhausted too much energy and have delayed my progressive move forward.

No longer viewing you as an enemy, but as someone who was directed to teach a lesson using tactics that may have appeared offensive, yet strategic and necessary.

Once you have fully realized how immature and damaging to the core it is to exhibit hate, you will learn to relax.

Never seek revenge on someone who has wronged you. They might not be conscious of their actions. Don't immediately assume it was a deliberate attack. Release your guard a bit and relax.

Even if their actions were distasteful and unwarranted, do not let them cause you to become scandalous and obscene. Let go of those emotions. Pardon them swiftly.

When did you become obsessed with tallying up all those hurt words and actions done to you by those you have come to despise? Time to erase and start clean.

Mistakes are hidden jewels filled with precious lessons to learn and then master. Eventually, causing growth and moving us along to the next stage of life where challenges on that level await. Do not be afraid to live.

Do not let past experiences and pitfalls control your present actions to the point where you cannot move ahead because of fear. Forgive and you shall be free.

Forgive yourself even if others refuse to let you escape from the clutches of their oppression. They are not the creators of your destiny and their judgment holds no validity or merit.

Friction will keep us apart and not enable us to connect and build a legacy together. Let's agree to more forward separately or simultaneously.

As much as I want to hate you, I won't. For you may not truly understand the magnitude of your betrayal.

Maybe when the tension subsides and pressure refuses to rise will I let you in again. Until then, please keep your distance and allow me to be.

The folks who you love the most have the privilege of causing the most pain with their lies and deceit.

We must refuse to walk with heavy hearts and heads held low because of the cruel actions of others. Take back your power over self and move into a realm of peaceful tranquility.

Because of your ignorance and misuse of language, I will not let your words cause me to abandon you.

Moving past the distrust was difficult, but it became easier to cope with months later. In order for me to love again, I had to stop loving you.

Chapter 3
Change

DEAR TRAVELER:

Sometimes we choose to move with the seasons as we alter our moods and ways of thinking and executing. Other times we are forced by circumstances to shift paths, as a survival tactic, in order to stay alive. Either way, evolution is a natural occurrence which takes place in all living things. The struggle lies in making sure that you are growing and flourishing in a positive light rather than self destructing.

Change requires us to be fully conscious of the paths we decide to journey along before making a step because we now comprehend the power of our behaviors and the repercussions or rewards they may bear. The hope is to move toward our goals without too many lasting side-effects.

Your mindset is trapped in the days of tradition. Not like they have no place in a modern world, but to the point where it's difficult for you to switch ideas and be open to others' ideals.

Each stage of life is a development, one where we constantly transform. Hopefully into someone more profound and not something mediocre and mundane that gives nothing back to the earth.

Your moods shift too often, even when it isn't a full moon. Various phases of dark tones and gloom. Try locating a central state where you could settle and bloom.

Stop claiming you are so free when you are afraid to be whom you were designed to be and are far removed from living out your destiny.

New beginnings leave room for new possibilities even though they bring forth anxiety. This is a road we must endure for anything good to occur.

Whether you choose to evolve to a higher level or remain stagnant, then move backward, its still your choice; even if the decisions were made unconsciously, they were still made by you. Stop blaming outside forces and take your power back.

Change involves being constantly consistent. It is the folks who are not productive and self-motivated enough to take control of their destiny who are afraid of change. They despise it because they are often forced to do so by circumstance, instead of pure will.

As living creatures, like all life around us, we evolve and eventually reach a level of heavenly bliss on Earth and beyond.

When folks observe the lives of others they often yearn to change lives. Witnessing them enjoying the fruits of tireless, consistent labor. Yet, they don't want to endure the sacrifices, patience, self-control and a humility that are needed in order to prosper.

When seasons shift, so should your perspective on certain ideals. Bring forth new visions, filled with eternal possibilities and promise.

The Most High has removed folks out of your life because they were unfit to walk alongside you and would have hindered your mission.

Sometimes we do not know why certain folks are placed in our life or when their time will expire. Either way, they come to teach us lessons needed in order to progress to the next stage; even when those assignments are a difficult task to comprehend and master.

Distance does not make the heart grow fonder. Instead it causes you to see things logically, and forces you to come to terms with life's realities.

No one wants to hear the constant voice of complaints, instead practice problem-solving skills and keep your mouth closed.

How do you expect to break down barriers when you are terrified to travel mentally and physically outside of the constraints that have held your lineage imprisoned for generations?

We are supposed to change, grow, and develop into whom God designed. Evolution is a natural progression of life--to not evolve is to wither and die.

Most people are literally walking dead. When they see how alive you are it reminds them that they are stuck in a chosen hell.

Most folks fight the flow of change. Instead, they act in a manner, which puts folks down with negative comments that plant seeds of doubt in their mind. This gives them power over us, which is crazy because they are powerless over their own life, yet long to control someone else's. Never forget: manipulation is a tool only devils use.

It is very reassuring to know we always have the power to begin again, no matter what.

Before you lay your soul down to rest and reflect on the day, ask yourself whether you did everything in your power to touch the life of someone outside of yourself, family and work. Did you circulate positive energy or were you so consumed with your own well being that nothing else mattered? Maybe you were the pusher of negativity. Either way, tomorrow is a new start; a chance for redemption.

Change is easy. It's being content, but not complacent, with one's choice that's the challenge. Consistency is the cure, but it requires the art of discipline.

Chapter 4
Empowerment

DEAR READER:

Some days, situations, and circumstances surround you from every direction causing us to feel trapped into believing there is no way out from under the turmoil of life's junctures. It is during these moments, one must search for those things that inspire us to continue on and rise above. Listening to music, meditation, reading, exercise and talking things over with close family and friends is what has helped assist me during these periods. What has worked for you?

Remaining Empowered and Strengthened during doubt is easier said than done. The goal is to identify where our strength lies and work to remain centered in that space as much as possible. When connected to your power, the chances of losing it become slim to none.

Surround yourself with people who are where you desire to be in life. Their positive energy will eventually rub off on you and hopefully encourage you to continue to transform.

Everyone is dealing with something; Enduring a trial, struggling to get through and eventually overcome an ordeal. Hopefully, learning lessons and mastering challenging tasks along the way, making the process more purposeful and less regrettable.

It is a proven fact; whatever we focus our attention on ultimately ends up dominating our life. What have you been spending time focusing on lately? Where have you been giving all of your attention?

No one has control over the direction you choose to travel. It is solely in your power to decide which journey will connect you to your ultimate purpose.

Why are you stalled at the intersection of life? Held in position by nothing but fear; unable to see the light of truth guiding you to a place of safety where a balance of peace and tranquility resides in a zone without insecurity or doubt.

Distractions are designed to cause a state of confusion and delay the process of reaching your destiny at the appropriate time. Stand guard of anyone who attempts to interrupt your journey to prosperity. Never let their influence stagnate your movement.

Everyone is not meant to understand. Just you, the creator, and those angels assigned to guide and assist you with fulfilling your purpose.

Everything has a positive outcome. We must become trained at thinking positively in all situations, which starts first with unquestionable control of our thoughts, eventually controlling the totality of our life.

No longer do we freely give others authority over our future or present. Neither do we give them access to rewriting our past experiences. At this moment we regain our power and use it as a guide to maneuver.

One could never truly walk into the light of love without knowing and accepting their ordained greatness.

You have allowed others to have dominion over you. Allowing their words to rule as you served. It's time to lead.

The investment in self always has the biggest return. Contribute earnestly to your ambitions, then in those around you.

No longer will I be denied the opportunity to reveal my excellence. For too long I downplayed my shine to make others feel adequate.

Easy access into your life must be suspended or immediately revoked from the eyes of others to view and in air to share. Especially, if their presence has not been beneficial, but instead have had adverse effects.

Once you truly recognize the potential you embody to be stupendous above all measure, you will never be able to settle for being perceived as inadequate or insufficient.

Continuously seeking validation from those who stare at you with envious egos of jealousy will not fill the void of value you feel. Honor yourself and rejoice in your own presence.

We will never prosper in the space of instability.

Still bonded by thoughts of the oppressors? Twisted lies that cause actions to be questioned, moves to be halted and dreams to be delayed. No feelings of accomplishment, yet there are moments of focus. Make them productive.

Can you imagine the next few months, years being full of blessings and prosperity? Close your eyes and see it. Wow, what a powerful vision! It's enough to make you smile and push forward with even more determination, focus and courage. Just knowing what lies ahead. Think beyond this moment and celebrate the whole.

The art of discipline is taking total control over self and not being moved to act by mere emotions.

Try your hardest not to give energy to the maliciousness others perpetuate. Remember, their goal is to spread the infection of hate amongst those who exude an image of wholeness and luminous truth.

Stay immune to scrutiny and instead remain high off of the medication of love. It's the only proven remedy of protection against their criticisms.

Having your spiritual eyes open and alert involves constant communication with your spiritual guide. Don't let your attention be diverted or heart disturbed.

Always check in to make sure your actions align with the purpose written for your life, not what someone deems fit.

Remain in right standing at all cost. Do not turn from the light. Never sacrifice one's soul for ill promises of fortune and fame. They are illusions and will ultimately lead you into the pit of darkness; Empty, unfulfilled, and lost.

Do not blame others for the conflicts you experience externally or internally. Instead, evaluate the energy that allowed negativity to be attracted to your being. Protect yourself at all cost from sly serpents that attempt to infect your kingdom and cause havoc.

We are a minuscule part of the ultimate plan, so stay humble.

Stop complaining about not comprehending because of your level of education or background. Challenge yourself to think! At least try to ignite the brain to work for your benefit. Lazy thinkers are worthless creatures.

You are highly qualified to rely on yourself.

Dependence on others is often uncomfortable because it requires a release of control.

Self-sufficiency is the epitome of freedom, but even free folks rely on others for community building and collaboration to raise and protect the village.

No one will continuously empower you to become extraordinary. You must be able to kick-start the light from within and continuously keep the ignition running.

Have the courage to believe in your tenacity even when cynics doubt your level of competence, savvy sophistication and the way you shift through spaces with finesse.

Do not be hesitant when living out your purpose and never deviate from conquering ambitions. Instead, be resolute with your movements and migrate with spirit and vigor towards the destination.

Chapter 5
Persistence

DEAR TRAVELER:

Life sometimes appears overwhelming when you are working feverishly to bring your visions into a tangible existence. It would be much easier to just give up on future aspirations and goals, let life toss you around, and settle for the mundane-But then you would be lifeless, empty and unfulfilled, unworthy to walk amongst the living.

Persistence involves pushing through those dark days when your energy becomes low and it seems almost impossible to press on and fulfill the goals that inspire you. Remember your accomplishments and applaud them, then keep moving forward "by any means necessary".

Even when the road appears to twist out of control, valleys get too steep to climb, and the end seems too far to reach in this lifetime, faith must keep you pushing forward with persistence and every fiber of your being.

Close your eyes. Can you see overwhelming prosperity, treasures of abundance, and sacred lands of peace waiting around the mountainside? Soon we shall feel its presence and eternally rejoice in its favor on our lives.

Everyone is not supposed to understand or agree with everything you say or do. If so, you are only living to satisfy individuals instead of a higher power and purpose. Going against the grain is not always pleasant, but always necessary.

Even though uneventful trials, keep on stepping forward. If and when you trip, stumble and fall, get back up. Shake the dust off your designer rags and keep walking toward your destiny.

Grace will always keep you from sinking too far into the pits of fire. We were set aside by the Most High a long time ago. Now is the time to walk into our true abundance.

Dare to imagine yourself as God looks upon you. Can you see how beautiful and royal you are? The priceless image you just saw should be enough to make you smile, laugh and race toward your destiny.

Grant me patience, endurance and humility. All are needed to endure and overcome the tasks that lie ahead.

The seeds planted in fertile soil have now begun to take root and blossom. Soon they will yield the fruits of your studious labor. Until then the practice of being diligent continues.

As you prepare to travel back into the "belly of the beast," remember to keep your armor on tight, your faith cup filled to the brim, and the communication line with the Most High open and clear of disruption. Only then will you be able to endure the perils that may lie ahead.

Do not be too concerned with the beginning of your creation or the end. Spend your time focusing on living a life free from sin! The rest of the nonsense means absolutely nothing.

No, I don't always feel like thinking positive about a situation. Sometimes I want to react with calculated revenge, but then I remember that it would take me off my path, so I don't .

We all get tired of the robotic task of daily life. We rise, we work, we eat, we sleep, then we do it all again until life ends. Although the days and years become mundane, we must continue on and play the game.

Sometimes we just want to quit. Retire from the life we live. Maybe start anew or simply do nothing. It could be because the task ahead gets hard or doesn't appear to amount to much. Either way, We must refuse to give up.

Chapter 6
Purpose

DEAR READER:

When I speak it is always, always in terms of spirits and energy, because I am Spiritual. I don't speak directed at white or black, Democrat or Republicans. Those things are futile in the larger scheme of things. My thoughts are on a much higher plane. I now comprehend the tricks that were designed to separate humanity and cause just enough division and conflict to keep the level of distraction high enough for folks to not pay attention, accept the norm and remain asleep.

Purpose allows one to move within the confines of man-made institutions designed with their own principles and ulterior motives without losing one's own mission and values during the process. Only compromising slightly and never giving energy to debating over trivial matters that don't threaten the ultimate design.

Life is full of steps to climb; sometimes they are steep and other moments they are a smooth stroll, filled with swagger in every bop. At the end of the day life is meant to be lived and enjoyed, so keep pressing on.

How can a generation effectively teach their offspring when they are ignorant and have not yet found their way? Lost souls should not lead. They are the problem.

Use your voice to echo positive vibes that will touch the depths of its receiver's insides. Those lost in the turmoil of confusion needing a word of encouragement. Those wandering in darkness searching for an abundance of enlightenment.

It is more productive and meaningful when we rise and greet the day rather than falling into it and playing catch up the rest of the week. Be prosperous.

Too much time has been lost contemplating the next move to make. Spending years wrapped up in hesitation and self-doubt with little faith. Move quickly toward accomplishing those visions you have foreseen. Only you can birth them into existence. They were tailor made for your abilities alone. If not, you will lose sight of them and be left with recurring nightmares of a life you should have lived.

Take the time you need to work through difficult circumstances, but don't let them unhinge you from following your rage and seeking your target. Remember to only give a small amount of time to friction, and then cut it off before it infects the whole of your being.

Maintaining ambition and the will for our life is always the main focus, even in the most challenging situation.

Know thyself on a personal, intimate level and in a spiritual nature, so you understand the reality of your existence.

As you enter a new season, move forward and greet the essence that lies ahead. Shutting the door to the past. Keys don't fit the locks anymore. A new home waits. Running towards your true destiny and never stopping until you have made it there.

Being desire driven sometimes means being able to identify when you are speeding too fast and balancing too much at the same time. A need to halt and recalibrate is sometimes the only option to regain balance.

Whatever road you are currently traveling along, remember that you chose it! If you realize you're heading for a dead end jump the curb immediately and create a new path before you crash and burnout. Stop pretending you are not aware of your situation.

Never be begrudging of someone who walks in their truth purpose with sagacity and a ton of humility, instead stand in their glow and maybe it will brighten your life.

Chapter 7
Encouragement

DEAR TRAVELER:

The need for immediacy is a constant reminder of work needing completion. The global community awaits the energy you were sent to evoke. Lives have been displaced because you have yet to deliver. It's time for them to be re-aligned. Fall into execution mode at once. Please don't feel as if you have to deal with a situation because you may lack in a certain area. Have faith and know you have the power to change all things. It's your life so live it as if you were never going to fail. Follow this truth and observe every vision you have become a definite reality.

Encouragement is one of those gifts that we are able to give daily and to everyone regardless of the race, gender, religion, sex, educational level, status etc. It doesn't cost or take away anything from us to show compassion and respect to others using the mere power of kind words. Try it!

When temptation and overindulgence falls upon us, let us do our very best to remain stabilized and refrain from partaking or delighting in deeds of self-gratification and debauchery. They may prove to be detrimental to your physical, spiritual health and growth.

Always exercise the strictest discipline, so you won't have feelings of remorse later; when temptation will most likely be at its highest peak.

Stay on your path regardless of how fatigued you get. Your days of tranquility are near. Then you will be able to rejoice in making it through.

Even though uneventful trials—keep on stepping. If and when you trip, stumble and fall, get back up. Shake the dust off your designer rags and keep walking toward your destiny. Grace will always keep you from sinking too far in.

Hold on to dreams and they shall come true. It's when circumstances have blinded our sight that we lose faith and become unengaged. Stay encouraged and in sync with knowing how the memoir ends.

To postpone or set aside achieving your ultimate purpose in life is to undoubtedly fail; which breeds nothing but resentment. Keep your priorities in order. You must remain first.

Never lose yourself in the wilderness as you attempt to lead others out and into greener pastures.

When circumstances have tripped you up, trapped you so movements are impaired, and you yearn to enter a place where pain doesn't surround you and troubles no longer bring darkness: Remember, dreams of a bright existence are often conquered by nightmares. Try to ease your mind by reminiscing over smoother times, when all things were sublime and life was fine.

Stay the course, your next work of art will form into something more magnificent than previously predicted. No longer will your future be viewed with blocked vision. You will finally see.

Don't get down on yourself when you evaluate your current position in life and it's not the setting you desire it to be. Understand that it's merely a stage; a scene in the performance of a lifetime. It will soon dim with the light in a flash.

You consistently work outside of the realm of due dates and deadline, yet wonder why you achieve at nothing. Dreams die when you dare them to live. Don't be ignorant.

Get thee away from ignorant evildoers who openly and secretly wish for your demise. They are intimidated by your passion, which brings forth a sense of confidence and wholeness they will never comprehend with their small minds.

Chapter 8
Faith

DEAR READER:

Troubles will only last as long as you acknowledge them as such. Change the way you view situations and your reactions to them will change as well. Remembering that we are the controllers of our fate, when we truly believe. The problem: we trust too much in Man and rely on him to make decisions that dictate our lives. One day, we shall wake up and understand the whole system whether Republican, Democrat, Independent etc. has its own set agendas, which NEVER line up with the plan of what is just, ethically and morally sound. So keep your faith not in characters who play controllers and act as gods in government.

Faith sometimes requires us to just believe with not too many questions asked and answered. This can be challenging and unsettling for most of us, but when morale is high, belief is reassured.

God gave you power and dominion over all things. It doesn't matter how hectic and chaotic things get, you are always in control. Remember this jewel and you won't give in to the forces trying to derail you.

As soon as you feel the concrete support beneath your feet shake a bit as if it's ready to give way and collapse, leaving you suspending in mid-air, stressed out and overwhelmed with panic, and worried about stability-Remain calm, Collect your spirit and keep the faith. This is just an unsuccessful attempt to remove you from your position.

Life is full of lessons to be mastered before moving on to the next stage. The challenge is to learn these truths without placing too much energy on trivial matters associated with your present level, because then you risk the likelihood of being left stagnant, complacent, and possibly depressed.

Focus on the execution of things, not defeat, as your conquer plans. For the journey, bring along loads of truthfulness in your stockpile to help guide you to the finish line.

God is love. He is light. He is pure. As long as we align with this energy the right thing will always be done in our favor and the results will be prosperous.

As you place your armor on to protect yourself from the evils of the day, remember to be slow to act in defense. All battles were not designed for You to fight. Most are meant to be ignored, for they add nothing to life. Therefore, they are purposeless and void of concern. Only go to war when it is absolutely necessary.

The principle of truth withstands all and can never be destroyed, although many fools spend their entire existence trying relentlessly to manipulate its natural form and use it to deceive folks into surrendering their power of free thought.

You complain of being tied down and on the edge of checking out. These are the moments when you must rely on a source of energy more powerful than you in order to conquer all hurdles.

Never stop listening closely to the prophetic words of positive energy waves. Follow their signs faithfully before they suddenly stop speaking, leading and guarding. Causing the earth to fill with silence, loneliness and confusion.

Leave them where they lay. No need for you to risk anything else to bring them out of darkness because they will kill you first, in order to remain in hell.

Nerves can creep in at anytime. Usually they arrive because of the fear of not knowing or having doubts regarding the truthfulness of something to occur. Push those feelings away with all your might. They are blocking the joy you soon will celebrate.

Try not to second guess yourself so much when you already have a snapshot of the future. Just keep doing your thing.

It is going to happen regardless of what they say or don't say, do or refuse to do; so keep doing you.

Chapter 9
Integrity

DEAR TRAVELER:

We are constantly evolving (at least most species are), so stop acting like you know someone you met yesteryear. Folks love to put others in boxes as if we are not complex. Sometimes we need to be re-introduced to the new, more developed and whole Self. Of course, this is with the optimism that most folks actually find themselves well enough.

Integrity exudes through everything we do once we walk in righteousness and truth. It is what builds character and unbreakable bonds that cements honest, loyal relationships. Having strong foundations built on solid moral principals make our being more complete

Always amazed at the level of passion folks exhibit when focused on the lives of those characters that "entertain" and rarely educate or uplift, but instead mislead with buffoonery. When will we get tired of being so gullible and easily distracted?

A righteous man gives without expecting, loves under all conditions, leads with conviction, provides at any cost, and lives without doubt or regret because he trusts wholeheartedly that his actions are pure.

Maybe there are hidden benefits in appearing balanced, strong and focused rather than admitting you are actually broken and weak; incapable of facing your truth and over-standing your fears.

Just because you spit words of truth, does not make you automatically, a righteous man.

Do not waste too much energy and time beating down locked doors. It is obviously not meant for you to walk down those corridors. Heed the signs and do not enter. It will eventually save you time potentially wasted.

Some paths we were not meant to travel because they do not align with your destiny. Therefore, we should not force our keys to unlock them. Select choices wisely and cautiously or uncover the evil of Pandora's Box.

Life becomes purposeful when there is a need to live, instead of merely existing. Actually standing on stable ground with morals planted firmly because you not only believe, but know the righteous path.

When family, friends or random folks are not thankful or appreciative of kind gestures of any measure, it makes them appear cold and unworthy of certain actions and thoughts. Folks should always be grateful in every instant.

No one owes you anything, so stop waiting around for handouts and take control of your life.

If you have not yet accepted the reality that your life will one day expire, it is impossible to live each day with purpose.

We all make sacrifices, whether consciously or unconsciously. They are usually at the expense of other things like family, career, education, personal goals, friends, spouses, spiritual wellness, health, and future, etc.The challenge is to be accountable and aware of consequences related to what or whom you ignore for the sake of another pursuit. Sometimes the sacrifice can be detrimental to the whole, making all the diligence a total lost.

Learn to master your thoughts and your movements will sing for you.

Be absolute when you decide and see what happens.

Chapter 10
Sympathy

DEAR READER:

Please conserve your tears of sympathy and retract your words of consolation, for I now reside in a land free of distress and disharmony. I call this place my eternal home--entrance of the blues is prohibited and I will adhere to the rules.

Sympathy does not mean you feel sorry or pity someone. No one aspires to come off as a judgmental elitist who patronizes those who grieve. Instead, it involves showing compassion and consideration for someone experiencing a level of turmoil. Simply being supportive and comforting even if you don't know or understand the exact measure of their trials.

Why can't love shine its radiance in the midst of gloomy skies and thunderous storms? Reminding us that we, just for a moment, won't have to shield ourselves from cloudy dismal days for too long.

Death is simply the temporary suspension of consciousness. Soon you will awake from your slumber and be greeted with acclamation and praise for a life well lived.

Some view death as the end of life, others as a commencement into a world much greater. Your perspective on the matter determines how you survive.

The lights do not fade when you die. In fact, they shine brighter to showcase the legacy you have left behind.

Pain is something we all encounter at one time or another. It appears in different forms on various levels.

Birth and death: The two things we know occur regardless of our actions. Since we all will one day perish, what shall we do in the interim? Live: The only part of life we truly have control over.

Grief is often unavoidable and to some, a daily way of life. Meditate on healing the heart before it turns gray or the beast takes control of the soul.

Depressed living should not take over.

Although the departed physical is no longer with us her spirits travels alongside us daily. She is the angel who has guided our steps and made each path clear and free from negative vibes.

How much more does one family have to endure in order to feel the loss of death no more? Is it simply a stage that teaches the value of life at an expensive price? Or do they always go hand in hand to balance the ultimate plan and keep order within the land?

Don't ask a bunch of questions when someone is dealing with strife of any sorts, just be in their presence and do what needs to be done to make them laugh.

No one wants to focus on the array of emotions they experience while dealing in sorrow. Instead, they would rather enjoy a touch of normalcy as they work through life's pit-stops.

It's often difficult to let people go when they have overstayed their welcome, but they must be removed in order for new energy to enter their former residence.

In times of lost we must try to see the possibility of days ahead that consist of less heartache and sadness.

Sitting in a sea of broken hearts whose worlds have joined by the lost of a loved one connects us to the realities of life and death.

No, I don't know exactly how you feel at this moment, nor can I comprehend your present whirlwind, but I'll be right here to comfort you sight unseen.

Loss or being lost, affects us all differently. Our wounds are even personally designed based on the extent of the trauma. Try not to measure your pain against someone else's.

Chapter 11
Patience

DEAR TRAVELER:

Was recently in a discussion where I lost my cool and became a bit upset. I realized that these little moments are a test of patience. I am continuously working on reacting slower. Expecting and appreciating that tests are placed in our path to teach us lessons, so we can move to the next phase. When we continue to fail these assessments we end up becoming stagnant and sometimes having to begin again.

Patience is not the easiest assignment to master for most folks, especially those living in a fast-paced digital age of immediate access. We must learn to be still amidst the noise and distractions of our surroundings. Listening to our heart beats and the rhythm of our breath as a guide while awaiting signs of our undeniable blessings. "It was written" and it shall be.

A rational mind thinks things through before acting and/or reacting. It is not moved by mere emotions or motives because it's disciplined, insightful, and wise. Self-control is its prize , not demise.

Getting overwhelmed is the spirit's way of letting you know a time of sitting still is needed. Delight in this moment of meditation and let the body heal.

As you evaluate your current position in life and realize it's not the setting you desire it to be, don't get down on yourself. Understand that it's merely a stage, a scene in the performance of a lifetime. It will soon dim with the lights and fade into the background.

Try to embrace this moment with grace, a smile, and a reassured sense of comfort because you never know if or when the lights will shine again.

You must continually and constantly strive for righteousness. Be a beloved brother or sister of perfection! Your journey doesn't end until you have reached the light of total understanding and wholeness.

The seeds planted in fertile soil have now begun to take root and blossom. Soon they will yield the fruits of studious labor. Until then, the work of staying tolerant continues.

Motivation and determination are great characteristics to possess, but moderation is the key. The wise action to take in this situation would be to step back, lighten the load and keep the faith.

Others may view your inactivity as laziness and sloth-like behavior. They have no idea that you were told to be still, so you can welcome your blessings.

Never was the type to rush through the tasks of life. I'd rather move slowly, so I can not only delight in the process of living but be sure to not miss a lesson or two along way.

Relax. Just sit, lay or stand right there in that very spot and space. Now just wait.

Ignore the voice that tells you to hurry up. Says that you are wasting time and need to "step on it because nothing is promised and no one will wait". Don't let anyone or anything dictate the pace of your movements. You decide with a clear head, heart and spirit when it's time to push forward.

Chapter 12
Hope

DEAR READER:

The yearning hope is that even in physical absence, these sacred proverbs continue to breed life and ignite positive transitions powerful enough for you to believe change is possible.

Hope only exist in the absence of pessimism. One can not expect to be fortunate and profitable when they are consumed in doubt. Don't let those thoughts arise and take root because they will block out the prospects of promise.

Although forces have plotted and conspired relentlessly to barricade this flux of energy, words of prosperity will continue to flow until the last breath is released or pen is inked.

What a privilege to observe the surge of will and determination folks exhibit days after New Year's celebrations have ended and resolutions are declared. I pray the same flow of energy remains with you throughout the seasons and whatever goals set are achieved without too many pitfalls, roadblocks or doubtful moments of confusion.

When you feel like your hard work just blew up in your face, immediately pick up the particles left in the rubble. They can be preserved and used to create a new life, beginning: masterpiece.

When someone continuously approaches you for a listening ear and a few words to help their mind clear, don't get to upset when you have to repeat the cycle again and again. Eventually the lessons will stick.

With these dark days appearing to be the new norm, hold on. Things will turn out in your favor soon enough. In these moments stay tough. Don't give up hope.

Realize that this is just a moment that appears uneasy causing you to second guess the decisions you made and the actions you take.

Hold on to the confidence that has welled up in you over the years and has helped you travel along paths that very few have been able to muster up the courage to travel.

Always know that your deepest, most intimate desires to be better in all areas and will eventually come to fruition. In the meantime, continue to prepare yourself to receive all that is coming to you soon.

No one truly knows if we'll even make it from under the clutches of those who continue to oppress free thinkers and callers of peace and equality, but we must remain optimistic.

Continue to look at others with admiration and expectations that even the most cruel person has enough love inside to one day flush out the hate that resides.

Belief that the essence of everyone you meet is ultimately good allows you to look past some of those discouraging behaviors and not let them affect your perception of them too much. Making your interactions a little less uncomfortable.

Learned a few years back not to totally despise the pessimist outlook of some folks.

Don't let them label you a daydreamer who doesn't have a handle on "reality" just because you are more hopeful than they are and have faith that a state of utopia can be reached.

Events will occur daily no matter what, some planned, others are unexpected. The task is to approach either one from a positive perspective as you search for the lessons and opportunities of growth inside each.

You have heard the saying, "goodness always prevails", but do you actually believe it to be true? I sure pray that you do.

If you are not hopeful that life will get better as we work each day a little harder and with more focus and determination to be better, then what are you striving for when you awake and travel on your way. What are you motivated to gain?

When the cynics and those with skeptic sneers attempt to scorn at you for being too enthusiastic about the possibilities of goodness found in all people, politely stare back at them and smile.

Chapter 13
Humility

DEAR TRAVELER:

Never quite cared for those who boast and brag about their accomplishments and/or accolades. It's okay to achieve and push one's self to be considered significant, but when you wear them as a badge upon first meeting someone it signals there are deeper issues underneath: the thirst to be validated hidden behind the mask of modesty.

Humility does not call for us to yearn for the spotlight. It actually causes one to shriek in bashfulness. Becoming more reserved because they are not seekers of fame, yet possess the confident and silent arrogance needed to transcend.

When something is for you, pure spirits conspire in your favor; regardless of what man says they can never have enough substance to yield the final word.

When someone approaches you with negative vibes and slanted, cross eyes look at them with the security that only a righteous man and woman can possess. For they may not have realized the magnitude of evil they attempt to spread.

Most folks claim to be alive, but are actually missing their hearts; therefore, they are walking dead, workers of Lucifer. Looks like they sold their souls for the mirage of fame and fortune. They have too much pride. Barely can look a righteous man in the eyes.

When you realize generations upon generations have walked the Earth at some point and have died and moved on, you accept the fact that you too are only living at this moment in time for a moment in time and will cease to exist.

Try not to wish for what you do not have. Become a good steward over what has been blessed to you.

Words arrive at our doorstep for different reasons, at different times, and from different senders. Sometimes the news enlightens and adds depth to life's experience, at other times it attempts to ignite bitter vibes. How we react to life's pressures proves the true test of man's pride.

The format for not losing one's soul to the illusion of fame and fortune is simple. Stay in LOVE; Love should be exemplified in everything we do, and everyone we touch. It will keep our angels in protective mode and ward off those evil spirits trying to infiltrate.

Never be envious of someone who walks in their purpose with confidence and humility, instead stand in their light and maybe it will brighten your life.

The confused look in your eyes that reveals you didn't comprehend those spoken words. Ignorance and ego prevented you from asking for clarification. Become more humble and open yourself to the unknown, then grow.

Why do some folks move their lips and force their voice to activate when they say nothing worthy of hearing? Regulate your words before you speak and save yourself the embarrassment of sounding ignorant.

Never take for granted the sacrifices made by someone who selflessly reaches out to pull you up from treacherous waters and onto safe lands. One day they might not appear and you will drown in loneliness, guilt, and regret.

A man always takes the blame whether right or wrong. He is the head of his family. If you can get down with his Mission, let him lead.

Most folks can read on some basic functioning level, therefore the problem lies with comprehension; It is what causes us to stutter and stumble. Eventually leaving one frustrated and confused.

Remain reserved in who you are and who you are becoming. There is a way to be prideful without boasting of your accomplishments.

There is a way to be assertive when speaking to folks about things that may be uncomfortable without coming off as being arrogant and pretentious.

Having and displaying a sense of humility does not make you weak or docile, it actually shows a level of modesty and respect that some are too shallow to portray.

Just because others are louder than you or flashy in their appearance does not mean that they are superior to you. They are obviously pretending to be much more than they know they are.

Refrain from attempts at being rude towards others because you find it easy to interact with those you view as being submissive and non-threatening.

Chapter 14
Commitment

DEAR TRAVELER:

Once we have set our minds on achievement on any level, we must then dedicate our actions and energies on the attainments of those goals. Chasing after them with strict focus, whereas we become consumed with nothing else. Leaving little room for distractions because if we lose sight of those visions, we lose our direction.

Commitment is the pledge we make to ourselves that we will stay disciplined in our conviction to stay the course. Towards becoming better than we were previously. It allows us the opportunity to test our sincerity towards change and overcome obstacles that will attempt to sway us to act irresponsibly ultimately breaking our stride.

Your time of being held hostage-by yourself-is well over due. Immediately pay the tab and quickly post bond so you can free yourself from past hurts, self-doubts, fears and disbelief. The moment you set yourself loose from this cage is the same moment you begin to live life on your terms.

Surround yourself with people who are where you desire to be. Their positive energy will eventually rub off on you and hopefully encourage you to continue to transform. Whatever we focus our attention on ultimately ends up dominating our life. What have you been spending time focusing on lately?

Never let folks control your actions or influence your thoughts by the ignorance they spit from forked tongues. It would be a devastating mistake to hand a fool power over your life.

The body, mind, and spirit have received the rest they needed in order to be effective. Now that you are awake from your slumber, get moving and do something productive. Try something different from your normal routine and watch the effects of your change in action, bringing you closer to fulfilling your destiny.

Close your eyes for a moment and open yourself up to the energy around you. When you feel the air grab hold of your hand and hear the spirit whisper in your ear, follow it. Let its power guide you to your blessings.

Time is of the essence. It is imperative that you seize the moment and reap the harvest that waits.

We have an unwritten obligation to ourselves and those who sacrificed for us to have the opportunities the lay at our feet, to be outstanding and to live above average.

If you have not done so yet, today is the day you take the pledge to begin and finish the goals you set sometime ago and even somewhat began, but never totally completed.

There is an old saying we used in my neighborhood when I was young, "word is my bond". We often used this phrase to signify that we were being truthful with whatever we were telling. Even then, we knew a man's word was his assurance.

A vow is an agreement between oneself or others that must not be taken lightly or for granted, but instead held to the highest standard. Once made, it is almost impossible to break. Or at least it should be treated that way.

Never be forced into making a decision until you have taken the time to review all of the guidelines and terms listed because once you sign your Hancock, there is no withdrawing.

Chapter 15
Wisdom

DEAR READER:

Not everyone needs to be trained and conditioned by an institution of higher learning to gain a depth of knowledge. Sometimes I lie awake in silence awaiting messages of light, truth and wisdom from the Most High. Eagerly, yet patiently listening for the spirit to speak to me and fill me with answers to the secrets of tomorrow, so I can better navigate my way through the day without interference or sorrow

We gain wisdom after we have spent time in reflection, study, and mediation. We have collected the evidence and have weighed options, consequences, and benefits of proceeding forward with life.

Never underestimate the power of politics and propaganda. They are one in the same. All things are calculated! Search for the underlying meaning in everything. Don't let the media dictate it for and to you.

A man who dreams and works toward those aspirations rather than just dreaming at the expense of daily life uses a certain strength and character to balance instead of letting life crowd out those visions.

Settling should never be an option, regardless of the age. You'll regret it later for sure.

Words produce Thinking, which then produces Feelings; in turn produce Decisions which will eventually produce Actions. Choose your Words wisely and your harvest will be fruitful and plenty.

Learn more and more, each day, to appreciate LIFE and all those we have been blessed to walk with in the journey. Never taking for granted that it could be our last moment together. Therefore, let's always live.

If you never practice, how do you expect to get it right? Seeking perfection at every turn can be a cause for never starting.

Being a workaholic and renaissance man by ancestry, I've always lived by the saying, "work hard, play hard". As I gain more wisdom with age, I'm realizing that severe consequences are associated with "playing hard" and will ultimately affect work and family; whereas the detrimental damage will wreck future aspirations making immature actions unrepairable.

Concerning social media: Please don't let the false likes fool you! There is nothing that can build your overall esteem and self-worth, but you. Stop depending on others to stroke your ego and validate your worth. Instead, focus and fix those broken parts you try so hard to disguise behind the guise of someone secure.

Our ideals comes from the family and the rest from the media. We live in a capitalistic society, which is driven by money and materialism. Working to get money to buy, buy, buy, has replaced God. We are totally backwards, but swear we are moving forward.

If we seek it and build atop of the old to design something more profound and innovative, we will shock ourselves with how powerful we can be. Pushing all things forward with a mode of newnes is our real creativity.

As we grow older and become wiser to the truths in life, we learn to speak calmly with humility or sometimes not at all, especially to adults whose hearts have turned cold from years of living without a soul or youth who have been abandoned and lead astray by elders that took back their trust in them.

Dinero, like knowledge can be earned. The difference is that money can be lost or stolen from one's person. Knowledge on the other hand, is not so easily diminished once acquired. If used correctly, it can bring forth an abundance of wealth that holds value over time and change.

They say some folks are in your life for a season or two, while others are blessed to travel alongside you sharing the sunshine and stormy days sometimes simultaneously. Know who's who and how their existence connects to yours.

Why don't they yet realize and accept that we are the few chosen? He needs to stay residing under our feet where serpents belong, not at eye level where they may whisper disbelief into our ears.

Your light will shine and you will be rewarded for your discipline. Remember, angels are with you and will react when you give them the signal, so use your words wisely and cautiously, the higher power is mighty and can shake down walls to rubble and blow holes through mountains.

Keep your eyes open and watch closely for those creeps waiting to sit in your seat. They are vicious villains that plot and plan when they think you are asleep. They will never have the place they desire because they are unworthy. Plus, their place is customized for them. They just haven't located it yet.

"Man was not designed to live alone". He depends upon the enlightenment, energy, support and inspiration of those surrounding Him and vice versa. We depend and need one another to bring about the change so desperately needed in the world.

Lazy folks with a chip on their shoulders are a distraction and nuisance. Keep them away from your cipher.

It's in our nature to be godly, therefore when not acting accordingly one is immediately thrown off balance.

How do you maintain a healthy balance of spirituality, family, work, school, and a relationship while chasing after your dreams and aspirations? Because they are connected, it shouldn't feel like one has to or is taking precedence over the other. Just stay true to your purpose and all things will find their secure spot in your life, without much friction.

It is not worth the energy to condemn someone who was born and still resides in hell. Demons consume their every thought and action, therefore it doesn't make sense to harm them because they are already dead.

Why would anyone consciously get lost just to be left in darkness?

Chapter 16
Renewal

DEAR READER:

Healing is admitting the diagnosis was accurate. Acknowledging that something is not healthy within us allows one to place attention on getting better, a priority that can not be ignored or set aside. It must be dealt with now.

Renewal relates to the process of awakening one's self to a new beginning. A place free from the destruction of the past that may have suffocated your growth and caused periods of exhaustion that almost caused you to retire earlier than expected. The hope and opportunity to literally erase the past and start along a new path is restorative justice.

Don't fear the moments when you feel alone, abandoned, and outcasted from the world. For this is a time of reconstruction and renewal. You will be made whole again in an instant. Greet this period of melancholy with open arms; don't fight it with clenched fists.

Sit when your soul gets weary. In a moment you shall rise again and continue with your life's work.

Stop living behind the weak excuse of "not knowing" as a reason to remain ignorant, stagnant, and unapologetic. Uncover knowledge then transform it into wisdom while mastering understanding.

Why are some of us so often attracted to broken birds? Can we truly assist in healing them? Or is it an undying need for our own significance to be endorsed?

We are always evolving to someone greater than we were the day prior. It is our right and duty to identify when we have out lived our former selves. In doing so, we start anew and take full advantage of a rebirth.

Pay close attention to the signals your body gives off. They come in the form of stressors, illness and other signs. These are triggers for you to take time off and recharge before you literally collapse.

When you truly wake-up, your senses will be restored to an acute stage of heightened awareness. Back to the time when you were the most consciously balanced and jovial. Where being was limitless.

The true awakening comes after you awake from a time of slumber and realize the reality of your existence.

This world will send you into overdrive, then consume your mind until it over loads, unless you take the time to disconnect and reboot.

Be aware of those who will remind you of your past experiences as you move toward creating newer stories that overshadow the darker days. They refuse to allow you to escape.

Stay surrounded by all the things and people that allow you to flourish along this new path. They are placed in your life to support you towards your renewal. Do not push them away.

Chapter 17
Peace/Tranquility

DEAR TRAVELER:

Reaching a level of zen and maintaining it for most of your days and life has always been the ultimate aim. Staying balanced and not being caught in the propaganda designed to enslave our mental and spirit so we forget what it feels like to be one will living energy that resides in everything around us. Losing the innate connection to the source of light that helps us grow, elevate and shine

Peace and Tranquility is a state of being that very few are fortunate to find and then hold on to for a sustained period of time. They are so engulfed in a life of constant chaos that they have given up searching for the truth. Darkness and damnation has conquered their soul.

Had to disconnect in order to walk with greatness. It was the most terrifying, yet gratifying thing. To enter the dark, then greet the light. Then stay there for eternity.

Never be ashamed of showcasing the new you to old friends and family. It will indeed inspire absolute, undeniable change in those who intersect your path and connect to your energy circuit.

Be forgiving and you too can rise from the dead to ascend into a state of heavenly bliss here on earth.

Unlimited freedom looks like time stood still and the only thing alive is the scene you are presently in.

Tranquility is a chamber where life finally makes sense; a environment where love stands tall as it replaces all.

Being in the Now feels like eternal bliss, especially when the mind is free to roam without apprehension or thoughts of past trials or future accomplishments.

It feels like a state of ultimate peace--A realistic snapshot of heaven.

The sun has been shining an abundance of energy even through the surrounding gloom of the day. In this we find divine peace and favor, which is being converted into freedom of life and expression.

During these moments of calm stillness and heightened acute senses, I can hear God speak. His voice confirms that he is pleased.

Freedom is acquired when moments of overwhelming peace are found. It is at these times, the chains of mental torture and confinement are released.

Enjoy the temporary emancipation from oppression.

When the work week has finally come to a temporary end, enjoy it as much as you possibly can, for the robotic days of performance will soon return again.

In the midst of all the madness, appreciate quiet nights when the world seems unconscious. It's the essence of divine contentment.

You are at a great place in life's self pilgrimage towards discovery. Enjoy the time you have with you. Only then will you be able to truly introduce yourself to someone.

It is extremely more difficult to strive for righteous perfection than it is to simply exist in a world of discord and pandemonium. It requires practicing until it becomes instinct-almost second nature. Then, when your higher consciousness opens and you view the world from a more spiritual, yet simplistic perspective-you have arrived.

<u>EPILOGUE</u>

First, you perform for others seeking acceptance and validation. Soon you realize man has faults and few live up to expectations of any sort. Then, you learn to achieve for self as a test of personal limits, forcing independence, and setting new standards. Finally, you comprehend how all is done with the sole purpose of pleasing a higher spirit: God.

Every other action is futile.

No one will have your best interest in mind more than you, nor will they ever fully comprehend how much you endured without succumbing to the pressures designed to destroy or de-motivate you towards your destiny. They are too focused by their own desires to care about yours.

I hope these messages of inspiration have found a special place in your life and have arrived at the very moment you needed them the most. I am merely a vessel and will continue to do my part with uplifting all seekers yearning for change and positive vibes.

Because I have been surrounded by so many positive folks I have been inspired. All of you are to thank for the words I have been blessed to share. You have in one way or another traveled through phases with me. Continue to be the voice of reason in your immediate and outer circles. Peace and Love, eternally. One!

Although it is my duty to act as the chef and serve the healthiest entrees to the hungry, what I have realized is that people cannot be forced to eat and some don't even recognize when they are being given a free meal to savor or even how nourishing words can be for an empty heart. Instead, they prefer to eat from the same slop pigs play in.

Personal Quotes from Some Supportive Folks:

Humbly moved by your comments of support and love. I just write about what I am dealing with at the moment, sort of a "self-talk" method of processing, then I package these discussions up to share with the world. I never know who will connect or if my words will fall upon deaf ears, but I disperse them anyway. I'm ecstatic to know you are and have been tentatively listening! Your encouragement persuades me to continue using my voice to spread positivity and inspiration to brighten melancholy days.

Theodore Ervin Jones

Your words have helped me with the power of listening-for it is a gift and grows as we grow spiritually. My son, life takes on new meaning when we just open ourselves to this gift of listening. You are one of caring spirit and I am most proud of you pushing people to be their best they can be.

Aiyana Rosales-Thomas

The quotes in this book not only inform you of how to live a positive life, but encourage the reader to look back on past actions to create a better future. The great thing about this collection is there are words of inspiration for anything you are going through.

Dorian Thomas

Your words are encouraging to me. They helped me look at things from all sorts of angles. It showed me to look at the cup half full instead of half empty. Your words filled me up instead of draining. Taught me to be brave and humble. They inspired me to be full of life and be positive no matter the situation. They helped me believe in myself and made me believe I can do whatever I want to do as long as I dedicated myself.

Kimberly Williams

Your words of inspiration helped me want more in life. You encouraged me to want to go to college, be a homeowner and to always remember that I am not the product of my environment. I've looked up to you. I wanted to be the female you. You always told me to know my worth and never settle. You're perfect in my eyes. You are just inspiring all around the board. I admire you because you beat the odds of a Black Boy growing up in the ghetto. I'm proud of you and will always support you.

Rashad Bradshaw

Words are very powerful because a positive influence can really nourish you in a way food and water can't. In my life, there are not many positive male figures who have made that impact, but my uncle Ervin has managed to carry the load. thank you for teaching me the importance of incense and that life is all about constant pursuit of knowledge.

Michael Collado

We are all emotional creatures. The tension we cause within relationships and friendships sometimes causes trauma to the soul. Pride is the biggest bully. Makes me feel weak, so I stray then find me a pick up with good vibes. I'll stay. Inspired from the the top of the dome Unc..lol

Kristen Hinds

Reading your words allows for entering a vulnerable space of self reflection and healing. It allows for the possibility of resurrecting and always knowing there is hope for a brighter tomorrow. These are truly words to live by; a guidebook to living one's fullest life. Your writing is truly edifying and regenerative.

Cleo Rodgers

There is one quote from my beloved Ervin that I truly love and has helped me gain perspective on others behaviors.."As much as I want to hate you, I won't. For you may not truly understand the magnitude of your words of betrayal". Words to live by and pass on to the up and coming generation of my family!! Mere words cannot convey the inspiration and impact your wisdom has on so many, but I will still say...thank you and I love you..FOREVER!!

Chantaya Greene

Come in. Make your mark. Leave a legacy. You made me think about the kind of professional I want to be, that I should Be. And to always remember that you're doing it for the kids. This rejuvenated my spirit and made me remember my purpose.

Trevis Thomas—I love you unc!! Keep going!

Shaheen Thomas-Thanks Unc! Your words always make me think outside the box.

Jermaine Speaks —Erv, you have become a successful man and have learned the value of picking up the bricks that others have thrown at you and used them to build others, instead of tearing them down.

<u>Shontay Rose</u>

Your words have been and still are the ember to my flame. Let me explain; that while I may have what it takes I still need an encouraging reminder, a walk down memory lane to continue to persevere and push forward. A raised hand in a crowd is at times all you need to continue to find your way. To me, you're my older brother whose words of inspiration are voiced thoughts that help keep me encouraged and motivated.

<u>Lucius Thomas</u>

I have always been proud to brag about your accomplishments and your education. It has motivated me to find my purpose in life. Continue to be a servant and pray for God to lead you in the direction he has for you even when others don't understand.

<u>Kevin Gittens</u>

In every relationship transgressions will create separation that can be permanent or temporary. However, forgiveness is the key ingredient for reconciliation. Why? It produces peace, joy, and leads you away from resentment, bitterness, growing anger, discomfort and negative attitudes.

Liddy

"No matter how bad the news, things will definitely get better" were the words given to me by Ervin when I received my excess letter. And boy did things get much better for me at my new school.

Carrie Anne Tocci

Ervin Thomas believes we all carry a bright light within us and if we focus on that we will always shine. His writing reminded me of this and gave me hope when I felt others were trying to extinguish my brightness.

Tasha White

Continue to be a great inspiration to the people who are fortunate to have you as a part of their lives, and never let the gas run out with attaining more knowledge and helping others grow by broadening their mind.

Jermaine Tucker

A true king has spoken: peace to all men that can (Understand) accuracy with words of (Wisdom) please take time to (knowledge) this: Peace God; Stay Sharp.

Javis Dortch

Heard you were the inspirational speaker on FB. I see why. Keep it up!! You always possessed a great spirit Erv! And always wanted so much out of life, I'm really happy that you had the courage to believe in yourself and give you a chance!!

Shanta Rodgers

Because of you bro, I took the time out to start with a self inventory that lead me to celibacy and gaining an intimate relationship with God! I can honestly say I love me and my fellow brothers and sisters unconditionally, without limits. And it is an amazing feeling. Listen to me loud and clear...I absolutely love you.God has placed you in my life and you serve your purpose constantly, clear across the map! It's like while I'm pondering, he whispers in your ear. THANKS AGAIN MY BROTHER.

Markita Roberson

Wow, I'm Speechless. You know how you go to church and when the pastor preaches you feel like he is speaking only to you? Well, that's how I feel right now!! I actually have tears in my eyes because this is so speaking to my heart.

Jaime Williams

Erv , I will pray for you because you are a very inspirational, wise, and motivated brother. I hope the world is ready for you.

Anita Raman

Your "words" are the best Erv and it puts things into perspective. Keep them coming and I love the positive energy you present. God bless.

Lakisha Rourk

You need to write uplifting words for a hobby or a living. I really needed to hear those words from someone who recognize how challenges will become a distraction. Thank you!

Daria Jones

Absolutely LOVE It!!!!! This is so true about most of us...we can sometimes be our own worst enemies...we doubt ourselves so much and think we can't do something that we actually believe it....I paid the tab on most things I was holding myself hostage...now time to pay the tab for the rest to be "set free from my own chains"...Dang brother...needed that made me think am I doing everything I can be or should be?

Zulay Hunt

I'll be ur #1 fan next to your kids and girl when you write that book! Very Inspirational Erv, You have to write a book.

G'Wani Beals

Erv, truthfully speaking, I can always depend on you for some comfort when things start to look a little gray with your quotes and wisdom. Thanks bro. Keep motivating the people. Love is love. Smooches!!

Hasaunnie Hilliard-Sims

Thanks Erv! You are everything that W.E.B Dubois strived for...He would be proud to acknowledge you as one of the elite!-- I Just Love It! Thanx a bunch for MORE OF THAT POETIC JUSTICE- You Are Always Dishing Up A Healthy Serving Of "Food for Thought"

Kamisha Sykes- Thanks Erv!!! A blessing as usual.

Kalimah Ahmad--One of the wisest things I've heard in a long time.

Tammy Jo Ford- I've got to borrow this from you...so perfect!

Carla Reed

The journey of Life brings so much pain. Being a wise soul connects great spirits together. Words always spoken through the heart. The structure of our foundation could never be broken, so our journey lives on through our wise children.

Michael Thomas

Your words inspired me to continue to move forward even if there was no one there to support me. Your encouraging words and relentless drive is the reason why I recently purchased my home and reacquainted myself with my musical gifts.

Susan Grigsby- The heart of a teacher and the soul of a poet.

Quianay Bennett - Seriously, you need to be published.

Tracy Rust - You are a true realist.

Darren J. Showtime Tinsley - My brotha you are a true wordsmith Continue to lead by example.

Akida Neal - Great insight!!!

Stacy Angela Williams—-Sending you love and light.

Latanya Williams Nelson

You have impeccable timing. I was just tired at the hospital & I broke into tears because I was so upset. You just made things so much clearer & made my day.

Veronica N Claudio Rios

I'm sure people have asked before, but have you thought about writing a book? You have wonderful thoughts that should be shared universally. For now, thanks for the free motivation. It IS appreciated :)

Jermaine Hardrick aka Gotti

The truth attracts. All the darkness in the world can't drown out light, but all it takes is a small candle in a darkness to keep you from wondering where you are going. Erv your candle shall never burn out. I can't see how it would, when the words you spread are internalized by so many to the point that they actually adopt a particular mindset or behavior, based on having just a thought provoked.

Tomeke Bouier

Blessings.. God knew what he was doing, when he put you in position...keep it coming... your presence is more than welcomed, it's appreciated.

Mean Wright

My Big Brother Erv has been one of the most consistent people I know who preaches and practices the art of being positive! Keep up the good work family. If I'm watching, just know a lot more are also! We all need that energy.

Lionel Peterson aka Life Focus

Yea bro print a few of those words up on some hardbacks and I guarantee you can sell them and they would be of good use.

That's Education well groomed. No question you are always in my prayers Bro!

Dwayne Wright

This is why I honor this young man ..... taking life's struggles and devouring every piece of knowledge and swallowing it whole to become the man he is today. @Emtruths, I love you Lil bro and words can't say how honored I am to have you as one of my brothers from another mother.

And who says living in the projects doesn't make men? Continue to keep pushing and striving for greater success peace and many blessings bro.

Corbin Beckles

Knowledge, you always spoke with stern advice regardless of how the truth was perceived. Never lying to protect someone's feelings even if you felt their actions were wrong and they didn't or couldn't see it at the moment. You always showed me that even during the most troubled times to remain positive. As I watched you constantly keep an optimistic attitude. I have observed you always go out of your way to support anyone that was struggling with their own issues and gave them sound advice to deal with their situation accordingly.

Since meeting you as a teenager, it's always been a sense of urgency to come to the aid of a friend or loved one that's in need of someone to talk with and lean on for guidance.

Knowledge, Wisdom, and Understanding would be considered an understatement if I had to describe any good quality trait of your character as my best friend. Continued Peace brother.

MEET THE AUTHOR

Ervin M. Thomas is a native of Jersey City, New Jersey who began his career after Ramapo College of New Jersey as a mental health clinician then an educator for the Jersey City Board of Education where he worked feverishly as a special education teacher with the city's "at-risk" population, those classified with having behavioral and emotional disabilities. Before burning-out, Mr. Thomas transitioned to Georgia where he instructed a different demographic of students in Roswell for the Fulton County Board of Education. After gaining a wealth of leadership, curriculum development skills and his M. Ed in School Counseling, he returned to the Northeast with the belief that his expertise and experience would be better utilized serving youth who were fighting against economical and racially biased odds.

Currently, Ervin fills the role of guidance counselor at the newly founded EPIC High School in New York where focus is on shattering the "school to prison pipeline" cycle that has derailed so many of our young men of color.

Like so many children growing up in the confines of the inner city, Ervin has endured his share of pitfalls that accompany life navigating through concrete jungles. Instead of falling victim to the pressures that too often plague these environments, he sought a way out through education, the creative arts and community service. His hope and motivation has always been to acquire a position where he could empower others struggling to define themselves within a dominant and oppressive culture. He is an advocate of utilizing self-evaluation and goal setting techniques that facilitate the process of stopping the replay button on past traumas and investing energy into creating and pursuing future endeavors.

He has taken a vow to continue selflessly dedicating his life, as an educator, writer, motivational speaker and counselor, to influence youth and adults to think, operate, and survive beyond "the veil".

Made in the USA
Middletown, DE
04 February 2017